SketchBook Pro Digital Painting Essentials

Create stunning professional grade artwork using SketchBook Pro

Gil Robles

PUBLISHING

BIRMINGHAM - MUMBAI

SketchBook Pro Digital Painting Essentials

First published: October 2013

Production Reference: 1181013

Published by Packt Publishing Ltd.
Livery Place
35 Livery Street
Birmingham B3 2PB, UK.

ISBN 978-1-84969-820-7

www.packtpub.com

Cover Image by Gil Robles (gil@roblesart.com)

Credits

Authors
Gil Robles

Reviewers
Ricky Mujica

Angel Acevedo .Jr

Acquisition Editor
Mary Nadar

Taron Pereira

Commissioning Editor
Govindan K.

Technical Editors
Iram Malik

Arwa Manasawala

Shali Sasidharan

Copy Editors
Alisha Aranha

Tanvi Gaitonde

Dipti Kapadia

Sayanee Mukherjee

Project Coordinator
Aboli Ambardekar

Proofreader
Katherine Tarr

Indexer
Rekha Nair

Production Coordinator
Kyle Albuquerque

Cover Work
Kyle Albuquerque

About the Author

Gil Robles is an artist/illustrator living in New York City. His clients have included Bloomberg Market Magazine and the Review and Herald Publishing. His watercolors have been sold to private collectors.

Although Gil's training as an artist has been in traditional media, he has spent a great deal of time exploring digital media. Currently, he enjoys using SketchBook Pro for his paintings and illustrations and for leisure. Gil has posted many demonstration and instructional videos on his YouTube channel, `grobles63`.

I would like to especially thank my wife, Karen, who took the time to go over everything I had written to make sure that what I wrote down was exactly what I meant to say.

I would also like to thank my mentor, Irwin Greenberg, who passed away a few years ago. "Greeny" taught painting at the High School of Art and Design in NYC. Without his guidance, I would never have gone on to finish high school and go to college. He was, and still is, a source of inspiration for many former students who took his classes in high school and at the School of Visual Arts, as well as at the Art Students League, all in NYC.

About the Reviewers

Ricky Mujica is a New York City-born illustrator and alumni of the High School of Art and Design, Parsons School of Design, and Parsons in Paris. He specializes in book cover illustration using digital media, and fine art using traditional media.

He started his illustration career in 1983 using traditional oil paints and made his first digital illustrations in 1997. He has hundreds of illustrations to his credit and has collaborated on the beta testing and creation of several user manuals for projects involving specialized, industry-specific CG software packages, such as TopoGun retopology software.

His clients include: Harper Collins, Harlequin Books, Bantam, Dell, Little Brown Books, New York Times, Daily New, Ebony Magazine, US Tennis, 7-UP, Scholastic Books, and others.

He has been included in the Society of Illustrators' annual shows on several occasions and has won several awards, including "Best in Show" at the New York City Art Expo.

I would like to thank Gil Robles for writing this terrific book and Packt Publishing for giving me the opportunity to review it.

Angel Acevedo .Jr is a Designer/Sculptor who currently resides in Los Angeles, California. Originally from New York City, he developed an interest in the arts at an early age. While in college, he began to pursue his interest in sculpture and special makeup effects, which later on lead him into the film industry. Currently, he is enjoying his work as a Graphic and Web Designer and, when not busy doing work for others, he enjoys working with various forms of digital media, such as SketchBook Pro, Adobe CS6, Pixologic Zbrush, and Maya to improve his skills.

He has worked as a Graphic and Web Designer for publishing companies in New York and non-profit organizations in Albany, New York.

I would like to thank the author Gil Robles for giving me the opportunity to take part in the publication of this book. It's been a pleasure seeing his generosity in contributing his knowledge and skills to inspire many upcoming artists interested in the wonderful world of digital art. It is my hope that readers will come away with a feeling of empowerment and inspiration after reading this book and enjoy working with SketchBook Pro.

www.PacktPub.com

Support files, eBooks, discount offers and more

You might want to visit www.PacktPub.com for support files and downloads related to your book.

Did you know that Packt offers eBook versions of every book published, with PDF and ePub files available? You can upgrade to the eBook version at www.PacktPub.com and as a print book customer, you are entitled to a discount on the eBook copy. Get in touch with us at service@packtpub.com for more details.

At www.PacktPub.com, you can also read a collection of free technical articles, sign up for a range of free newsletters and receive exclusive discounts and offers on Packt books and eBooks.

http://PacktLib.PacktPub.com

Do you need instant solutions to your IT questions? PacktLib is Packt's online digital book library. Here, you can access, read and search across Packt's entire library of books.

Why Subscribe?
- Fully searchable across every book published by Packt
- Copy and paste, print and bookmark content
- On demand and accessible via web browser

Free Access for Packt account holders

If you have an account with Packt at www.PacktPub.com, you can use this to access PacktLib today and view nine entirely free books. Simply use your login credentials for immediate access.

Table of Contents

Preface

Imagine having all your painting and drawing tools in one handy kit. All of your brushes, paints, markers, rulers, and so on in one easy-access paint box. SketchBook Pro is that kit, packed with tools, brushes, and different media options. It is an intuitive program that allows the user to create professional artwork that mimics the look of traditional drawing and painting mediums.

What this book covers

Chapter 1, An Arsenal of Tools, gives an overview of the tools available in SketchBook Pro.

Chapter 2, Setting Your Preferences and Customization, discusses the customization of the software for optimal performance and ease of use. It also discusses the Do-It-Yourself Brush tool feature in SketchBook Pro.

Chapter 3, Creating an Image using Pen, Ink, and Color, focuses on the tools used to create a pen and ink drawing and how to color it. There will also be a demonstration on importing and coloring a scanned drawing.

Chapter 4, Creating a Painting, shows two demonstrations: first, a digital oil sketch demonstration and then a demonstration on painting a figure with the background fully rendered.

Chapter 5, File Saving Options, goes over the file saving options and how to choose the best one for your image.

Chapter 6, Tips and Tricks, gives you practical advice and helpful tips for using SketchBook Pro and continuing to learn about the software.

The bonus chapter, *Gallery of Images*, is an additional chapter containing a gallery of images created in SketchBook Pro along with a brief description and it can be downloaded from the PACKT website at the following link: http://www.packtpub.com/sites/default/files/downloads/8207OT_Gallery.pdf.

What you need for this book

- **Software**: Autodesk SketchBook Pro 6
- **Windows**: The following are the requirements for Windows:
  - ° Microsoft Windows 7 or Windows XP
  - ° 1 GHz Intel or AMD processor
  - ° 1GB of RAM
  - ° A graphics card capable of 1,024X768 display with 128 MB RAM
- **Mac**: The following are the requirements for Mac:
  - ° Apple Mac OS version 10.6, 10.7, 10.8
  - ° 1 GHZ Intel-based CPU
  - ° 1 GB RAM
  - ° Graphics card capable of 1,024X768 display with 128 MB RAM
- **Tablet**: The following is the requirement for a tablet:
  - ° A pressure-sensitive tablet and pen

Who this book is for

This book is intended for two types of artist. The first is the traditional artist with little or no training in digital media, looking to learn about an application that is both, easy to use and capable of producing professional quality work. The second is the intermediate digital artist looking to add to their knowledge and training.

Conventions

In this book, you will find a number of styles of text that distinguish between different kinds of information. Here are some examples of these styles, and an explanation of their meaning.

Code words in text are shown as follows: "For instance, the **Width** here is set at 4000 pixels and the **Height** is set at 3075 pixels."

New terms and **important words** are shown in bold. Words that you see on the screen, in menus or dialog boxes for example, appear in the text like this: "On the menu bar select **Edit | Preferences | Canvas**".

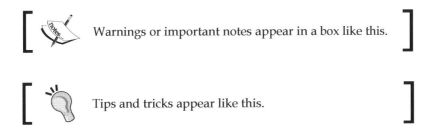

Warnings or important notes appear in a box like this.

Tips and tricks appear like this.

Reader feedback

Feedback from our readers is always welcome. Let us know what you think about this book—what you liked or may have disliked. Reader feedback is important for us to develop titles that you really get the most out of.

To send us general feedback, simply send an e-mail to feedback@packtpub.com, and mention the book title via the subject of your message.

If there is a topic that you have expertise in and you are interested in either writing or contributing to a book, see our author guide on www.packtpub.com/authors.

Customer support

Now that you are the proud owner of a Packt book, we have a number of things to help you to get the most from your purchase.

Downloading the color images of this book

We also provide you a PDF file that has color images of the screenshots/diagrams used in this book. The color images will help you better understand the changes in the output. You can download this file from: http://www.packtpub.com/sites/default/files/downloads/8207OT_ColoredImages.pdf

Errata

Although we have taken every care to ensure the accuracy of our content, mistakes do happen. If you find a mistake in one of our books—maybe a mistake in the text or the code—we would be grateful if you would report this to us. By doing so, you can save other readers from frustration and help us improve subsequent versions of this book. If you find any errata, please report them by visiting http://www.packtpub.com/submit-errata, selecting your book, clicking on the **errata submission form** link, and entering the details of your errata. Once your errata are verified, your submission will be accepted and the errata will be uploaded on our website, or added to any list of existing errata, under the Errata section of that title. Any existing errata can be viewed by selecting your title from http://www.packtpub.com/support.

Piracy

Piracy of copyright material on the Internet is an ongoing problem across all media. At Packt, we take the protection of our copyright and licenses very seriously. If you come across any illegal copies of our works, in any form, on the Internet, please provide us with the location address or website name immediately so that we can pursue a remedy.

Please contact us at copyright@packtpub.com with a link to the suspected pirated material.

We appreciate your help in protecting our authors, and our ability to bring you valuable content.

Questions

You can contact us at questions@packtpub.com if you are having a problem with any aspect of the book, and we will do our best to address it.

1
An Arsenal of Tools

SketchBook Pro 6 has a great selection of tools and brushes to create your artwork. It also has a number of places in the software where you can locate your tools. This allows the user to work comfortably and quickly while enjoying a great number of options. The following is an overview of some of the essential tools in SketchBook Pro 6.

Lagoon

There are several places to locate your tools and menu choices in SketchBook Pro 6. Like all computer software, you will find a menu bar atop SketchBook Pro. In the menu bar, you can access all your tools to edit your preferences or your document. SketchBook Pro also has a number of ways in which you can quickly locate your tools without having to continually open and close the windows or going to your menu bar. The following screenshot shows the lagoon window:

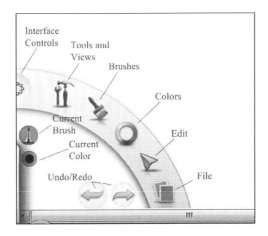

In the real world, an artist has a studio where all his equipment is stored—paints, pencils, markers, brushes, and so on. When an artist decides what to work on, he/she chooses the appropriate materials for the piece, or if he/she goes out to paint, he/she selects only the materials that are going to be used. The menu bar is similar to your studio, and the lagoon is similar to a portable art box where you keep the tools you use the most. The advantage of this is that you have several ways of arranging your workspace according to what is comfortable or expedient for you. Apart from the menu bar and windows such as **Brush Palette**, **Tool Box**, and **Colors**, you have the lagoon, as shown in the preceding screenshot, on the lower left-hand side of the interface.

The first set of menu options on the lagoon is called **Interface Controls**. This allows you to set up your workspace. You can set the lagoon to the left of your screen (it is on the left by default) or move it to the right. It allows you to take these elements off in order to use your entire screen to work on your drawing or painting. It also allows you to set up as many elements as you want on your screen when you are working. Any or all of the elements can quickly be brought back to view on your screen using Interface Controls.

The second set of menu options is **Tools and Views**. Here you have many of the options that are available in your toolbar. It is possible to customize your lagoon in order to place the tools that you use the most. In this way, you can have them readily available and can have your toolbar removed from view to have more space to work (customization will be covered in the next chapter). One of the default choices is Zoom/Rotate/Move Canvas. In order to activate the rotate canvas capability, you will have to set it up in your program preferences. You must go to the **Edit** menu on the menu bar, and then choose **Preferences**. On the **General** tab, go to **Graphics** and check **Enable Rotate Canvas**. (Note that right under this, there is a notice asking you to turn this feature off if you experience slow performance.) After you check the box, you must restart the program and the rotate canvas feature will start working.

The other default choices in your Tools and Views menu are Fit to View, Ruler, Ellipse, Layers, Symmetry X, Symmetry Y, and Actual Size.

You will find that when you start drawing, it is important to first choose Fit to View so that you can see the proper size of the canvas. Without selecting Fit to View, your image will occupy a very small area of the canvas.

The next set of options is **Brushes**. The default choices are Pencil, Airbrush, Paintbrush, Hard Eraser, Brush Palette, Ballpoint Pen, Swap Brushes, and Marker. Swap Brushes is a feature that allows you to swap the current brush you are using with the one that you have previously used without opening the **Brush Palette** window to look for it. For instance if you are using the Pencil brush and then selecting Eraser from **Brush Palette**, instead of opening and closing the **Brush Palette** window to get back to your previous brush, you can select Swap Between 2 Brushes in the lagoon and it will swap back to Pencil. You can do this with any two of your brush options.

Next we have **Colors**. You can select the colors you want to use from here. Most of your choices on the lagoon can be customized. You can either use these default colors or change them to the colors you use most often.

Next is the **Edit** options. The Edit option consists of the following options: Select tool, Lasso tool, Clear, Copy, Paste, Cut, Crop to Selection, and Move/Rotate/Scale Layer.

Lastly, there are the **File** options. The Previous Image option allows you to switch to the previous file in your directory. To the right of this option, there is a similar icon with an arrow pointing toward the right. This is for the next image in your directory or folder, in which you save your image files generated from this program.

The other features on the lagoon are inside the oval. There is an icon for the current tool brush you are using and also an icon for the current color. Selecting either one of these, opens the **Brush Palette** or the **Color Editor** window respectively. There are also Undo and Redo icons.

Toolbar

All the tools in the lagoon can also be found on the toolbar. There are more tool options in the toolbar, which can be added to the lagoon. The default tool choices in the lagoon can be customized to include only the tools that you use the most. In this way, you can work with only a few windows open and this can free up your workspace.

Going from left to right on the toolbar, you have the tools such as Undo, Redo, Select, Lasso Select, Crop, Zoom/Rotate/Move Canvas, Add Text Layer, Move/Rotate/Scale Layer, Ruler, Ellipse, French Curve, Symmetry X, Symmetry Y, Free, Steady Stroke, Line, Rectangle, Polyline, Oval, Layers, Brush Palette, Colors Editor, and Copic Library.

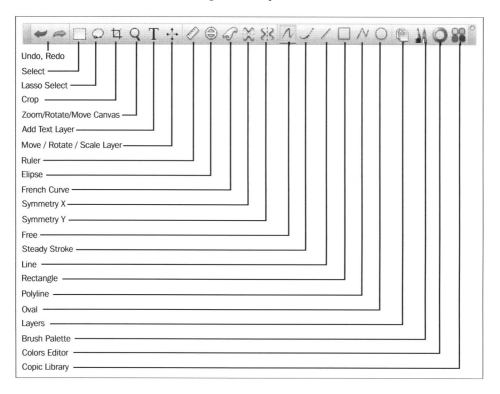

A lot of these tools are similar to what you find in many graphics software, and others have been on the previous versions of SketchBook Pro. Here you will be given an overview of the newer and unique tools.

The Ellipse tool

This tool allows you to make perfect ellipses by changing the scale and rotation to fit your design. When you select the Ellipse tool, a diagram of the tool becomes visible on your canvas. On this diagram or guide, there are icons that allow you to scale, rotate, and move the tool to accommodate your design. You can adjust the Ellipse tool to draw the shape you want anywhere on the canvas, and the line will automatically snap to the guide.

The Symmetry tools

The Symmetry X (horizontal) and Y (vertical) tools will place an axis line based on the tool you choose, and whatever you draw on one side of this axis will be mirrored on the other.

French Curve

This tool operates similar to the Ellipse and Ruler tools; however, there is a small icon at the very top of the guide that allows you to change the shape of the guide. There is a library of French curves and clicking on the icon changes its shape. You can also rotate and scale the guide similar to the Ellipse and Ruler tools. The following screenshot shows the French Curve on the canvas:

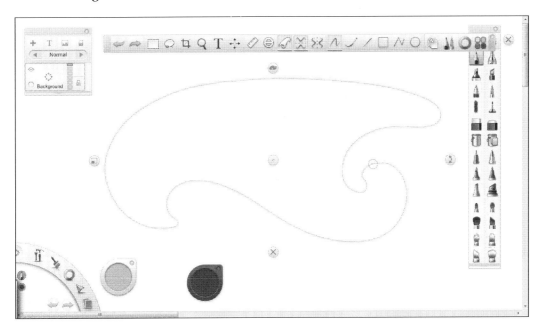

Steady Stroke

This tool allows you to make a steady and smooth stroke by dragging the line using a tether to guide it more accurately.

Lastly, at the end of the toolbar, there are icons that open up different windows or palettes.

The Layers editor

Just like any other graphics program, you have layers to work on. As you can see in the following screenshot, the layers in SketchBook Pro 6 are similar to the layers in other programs. You can add layers, change their transparency, or rearrange the layer order. There are two important features of the layers: blend mode and lock layer.

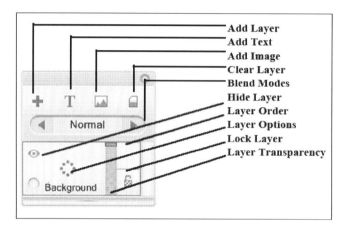

Blend modes

The **Blend modes** are similar to those in other programs, but it will be useful to go over them again here. The various modes are as follows:

- **Normal**: In this mode there is no blending taking place between any of the layers. **Normal** means that what is underneath the layer will be drawn or painted over and lost from sight unless one of the blend modes is applied.

- **Screen**: This mode ignores the black color in the layers below and brightens all the other colors.

- **Add**: This mode is similar to **Screen** but the colors become brighter.

- **Multiply**: This mode is opposite of **Screen** and **Add**. It ignores the white color in the layers below and darkens the other colors.

The following two screenshots illustrate the **Normal** blend mode. The first screenshot shows the value squares placed over a blue background. In the **Normal** blend mode, the value squares cannot be seen when the blue layer is placed on top.

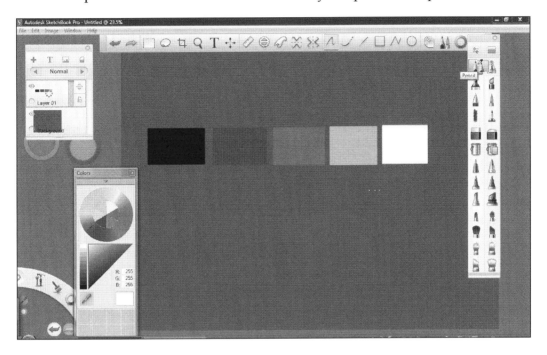

In the following second screenshot, the layer with the squares is placed below the blue layer. In the **Normal** mode, you will not be able to see the squares through the blue layer.

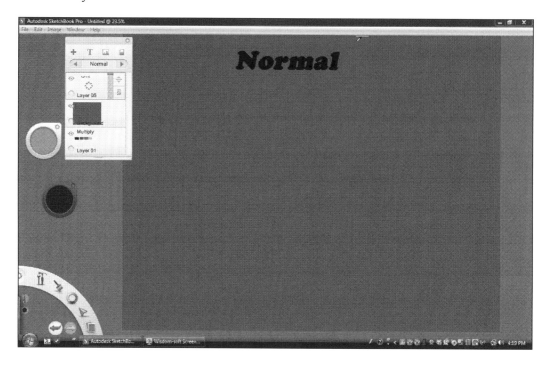

In the **Screen** blend mode, the black value square is ignored but the white and other value squares show through. They appear brighter because it adds white to the values creating a tint that blends with the layer color on top, as shown in the following screenshot:

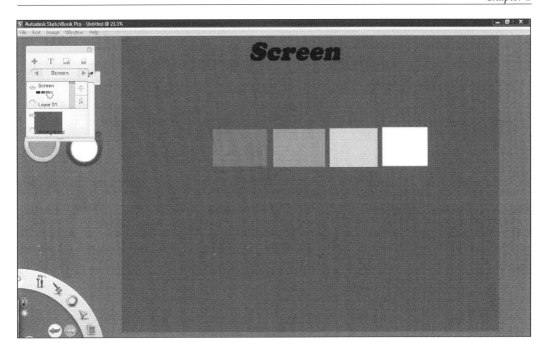

In the **Add** blend mode, the value squares appear as they do in **Screen**; however, they are brighter as seen in the following screenshot:

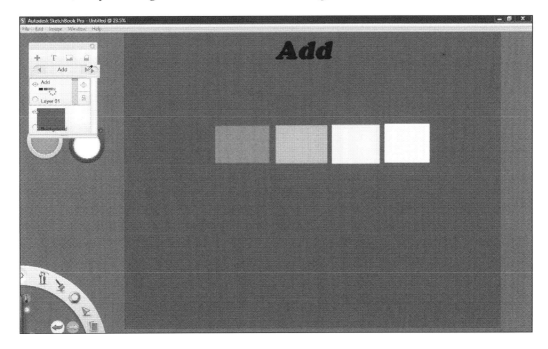

The **Multiply** blend mode is the opposite of **Screen**. **Multiply** ignores white and allows for the other value squares to show through, which are darkened because black is added to the values creating a shade that blends with the layer color on top.

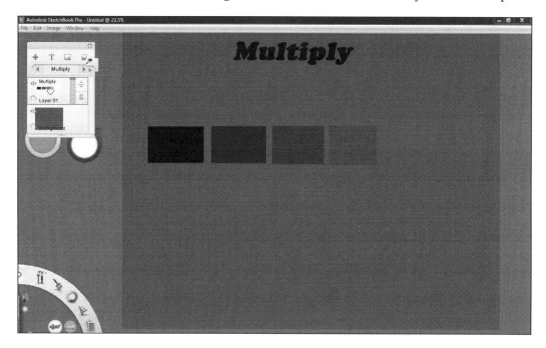

By selecting the Add Image icon, as shown in the following screenshot of the Layers editor, you can select an image from your image library and bring it onto the canvas:

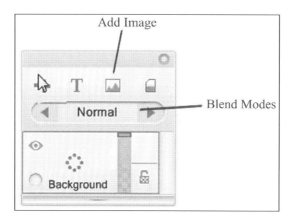

The dinosaur drawing in the next screenshot was originally done in pen and ink, then it was scanned and saved as a JPEG image in Photoshop.

If you place a layer underneath it and attempt to color the image, SketchBook Pro will still read the white areas as solid. so the colors will not show through as illustrated in the following screenshot:

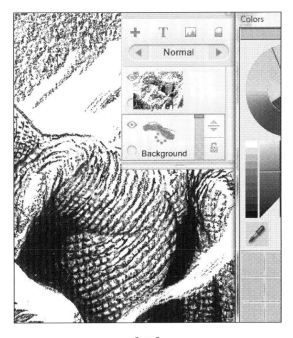

When you select **Multiply** in the blend modes on the Layers editor, the white areas are ignored and the colors in the layers below will be shown through as seen in this following screenshot:

In the following screenshot, another layer is added underneath the line art and the **Screen** blend mode is selected. This has the effect of lightening the pixels underneath when you color on this layer.

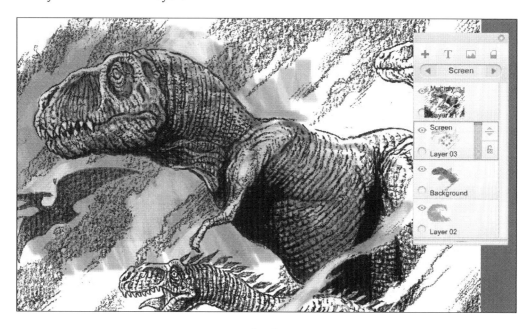

Lock Layer

When you work on an image, it is good practice to work on several layers separating the different elements of the image. This helps because if there are changes to be made, you can make those changes in the areas that you need to without affecting the other elements of the image that were placed on a different layer. Once you choose to lock a layer by clicking on Lock layer, as shown in the following screenshot, only the elements or the areas covered in that layer will be affected by the changes. For instance, if you were to separate line art and colors into different layers, and you decide to change the color of your line art, simply select that layer and lock it by clicking on the icon on the lower right-hand side corner of that layer. Now, you can change the color of the line art without affecting the areas around it. If you were to use color outside your line art, it would not show on your canvas because only the areas that were already drawn would change.

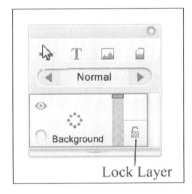

By selecting Add Image, a line drawing can be imported into SketchBook Pro, as in the following screenshot. A layer can be placed underneath to add background color.

Let's select the Lock Layer option in the Layers editor. While coloring on the layer with the line art, only the areas with art on it are affected as seen in the following screenshot. The area around the lines remains unchanged.

Brush Palette

The brushes are stacked into two columns, as shown in the following screenshot, on the right. These columns can be dragged up and down to select the wide variety of brush options offered by SketchBook Pro 6. On the top-left of **Brush Palette** is the Show Brush Properties icon, and on the top-right is the Show Brush Library icon that opens the brush library to view all your brush choices. You can customize your brushes in the brush properties window. You can also create your own brush by using the Do-It-Yourself Brush icon. (Customizing the brushes and creating a brush will be covered in *Chapter 2, Setting Your Preferences and Customization*.)

You can resize the brush that you are using without opening the brush properties. Tap and drag your cursor over the brush puck to resize the brush. Dragging it to the left will decrease its size and dragging to the right will increase its size. The brush puck is the light gray-colored puck shown in the following screenshot:

The Color Editor

A unique feature in SketchBook Pro is the color puck. The Color Editor works in unison with the color puck. Instead of opening and closing the Color Editor, you can tap on the color puck to access the color wheel where you can change the color. On the color puck, you can also tap and drag your cursor to left and right to change the saturation and up and down to change the brightness. The Color Editor is shown in the following screenshot of the palette with the color wheel, gray scale, and color picker.

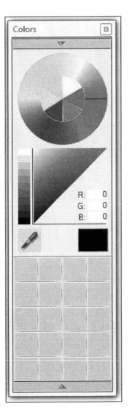

The color puck is shown in the following screenshot:

The color wheel in the color puck also contains a color picker, as shown in the following screenshot, which can be used to select a color that you've already placed on the canvas:

The color and brush pucks can be closed by clicking on the small dot in the top right-side of the pucks. To open them again, you can go to the menu bar, select the window, and then select the puck you wish to bring back onto your screen.

Copic Library

This color library is based on the popular copic markers used by cartoonists and illustrators and is especially popular among the manga artists. The following screenshot shows the window for **Copic Library**. The colors are arranged in two color sets, one for **Illustration** and the other for **Design**. The current color is displayed with the complementary colors underneath it. You can use the copic markers (which are the markers found in your **Brush Palette**) without having to open the **Copic Library** window. You can select the marker colors using **Colors Editor**.

At the bottom of the library, there is a space to drag the color swatches to create a custom set.

Summary

Although SketchBook Pro has plenty of tools, you don't need to understand all of them at once to get started. As you use the program, you will easily become familiar with all the options. As shown, there are many places to find these tools, so you don't have to worry about opening a specific tab to find your favorite tool or brush. In the next chapter, we will discuss how to tweak the properties on these tools as well as set preferences and customize SketchBook Pro.

2
Setting Your Preferences and Customization

When you start drawing in SketchBook Pro, you will notice that the images are a bit fuzzy; not clean and crisp. You will see this especially when you zoom in on your image. If you are going to print your images, it's important to set the canvas and image preferences to ensure the quality of your images.

Canvas

In the menu bar, go to **Edit | Preferences | Canvas**. In the pop-up window shown in the screenshot, you will see that the default width, height, and resolution settings are too low.

When you zoom in on an image with these settings, that image will pixelate, and when you print the image, the quality of the print will be very poor.

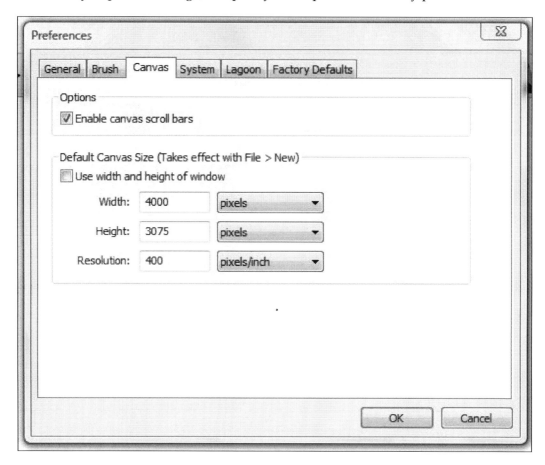

Set the height and width corresponding to the shape that you want—either rectangular or square. For instance, **Width** here is set at 4000 pixels and **Height** is set at 3075 pixels. The canvas area is more or less square shaped. The closer the numbers are to each other, the more square shaped your canvas area will be. It is recommended that at least one side should be set to no fewer than 4000 pixels as shown in the next screenshot. Also, the **Resolution** per inch should be set to no less than 400. By doing this, you change the default settings for the canvas. This will be applied every time you open a new document. The new settings will ensure better quality for the image and its print. Once you select the new settings, you need to open a new document for them to be put into effect.

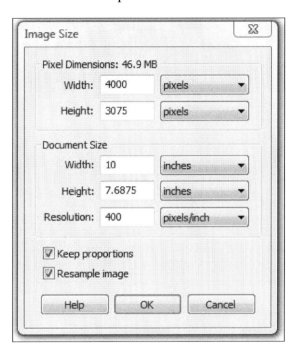

These settings can be modified for the current document you are working on without changing the default settings. In the menu bar, go to **Image** and then click on **Image Size**. The pop-up window that you just saw in the previous screenshot will appear on your screen. **Pixel Dimensions** gives you the canvas size as well as the total size of the document in megabytes. **Document Size** gives you the print size of your image in terms of height, width, and resolution. All this information is important in order to set up your document corresponding to its intended use. If you intend to print your image, you can set the document size to the final physical print size and specify the resolution of the image. If you are using your image on the Web, you can adjust your pixel dimensions which give you the actual size of the digital document. If you uncheck the **Resample image** checkbox, you can change the document size of the image independently from the pixel dimensions so that whatever changes are made to its height, width, and resolution will not affect the file size (in megabytes) which will remain the same.

It's important to note that the image size is independent from the canvas size. Image size represents the height and width of the physical document. Go to the menu bar and select **Image**, then select **Image Size**; you will see, on the window, the **Canvas Size** as well as the **Image Size**. Set the **Image Size** corresponding to the area you want it to occupy when printed.

Before you begin to work on your image, always select **Fit to View** in your Lagoon menu as shown in the previous screenshot. If you begin to work without doing this, you will only be working in a very small area of your total canvas. The final image will be very small. When you select **Fit to View**, you will see the entire canvas at once and you will be able to use and fill the entire canvas with your image.

Brushes

Every brush in your brush palette can be tweaked using the brush properties icon shown in the following screenshot:

Not all of the brushes have the same number of choices though. In the next screenshot, you will see the **Brush Properties** window for the **Pencil** and **Felt Pen** brushes side-by-side. You can see that you have more options to tweak in the **Felt Pen** brush window than the **Pencil** brush window.

Your full set of choices include: **Brush Radius & Opacity, Brush Color, Brush Advance Properties**, and **Brush Texture**.

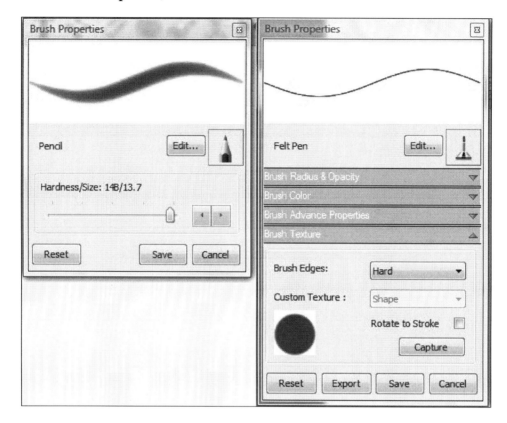

Do-It-Yourself Brush

You can explore a full set of brush properties by setting up a Do-It-Yourself Brush as follows:

1. Select the brush library by clicking on the icon at the upper-right corner of the brush palette. At the upper-right corner of the dialog box, you will see a small ring of dots as shown in the following screenshot:

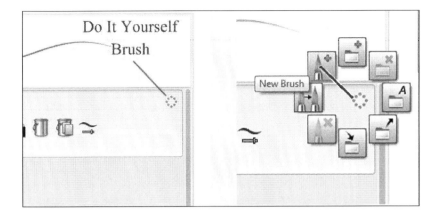

2. Click on the icon at the upper-right corner of the dialog box and select **New Brush** from the given choices.

3. The **Create Do-It-Yourself Brush** window will pop up on your screen as shown in the following screenshot:

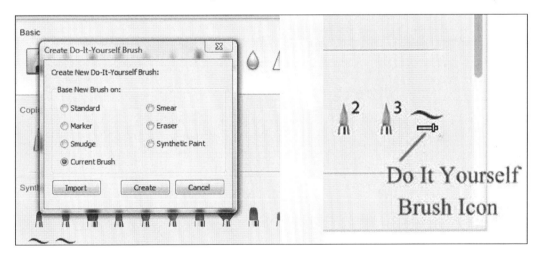

4. Select a brush type and then click on the **Create** button. A new icon will appear in the brush library. Double-click on the icon to edit the properties of Do-it-Yourself Brush.

5. In the **Brush Radius & Opacity** section shown in the following screenshot, use the sliders to adjust the opacity and size of your brush stroke. The size and opacity controls refer to the appearance of a brush stroke when heavy or light pressure is applied to your stylus.

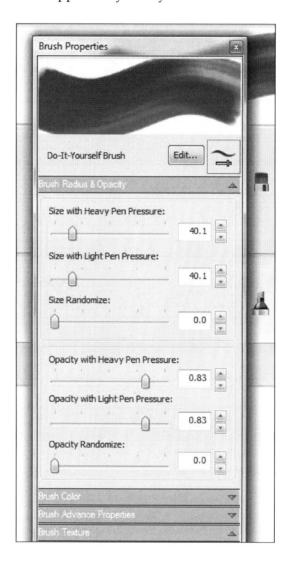

6. The **Brush Color** setting allows you to randomize the hue (color), saturation (value of the color), and brightness of your brush stroke. This allows you to add unpredictable special effects in your image. In the following screenshot, you can see the effects of these settings applied:

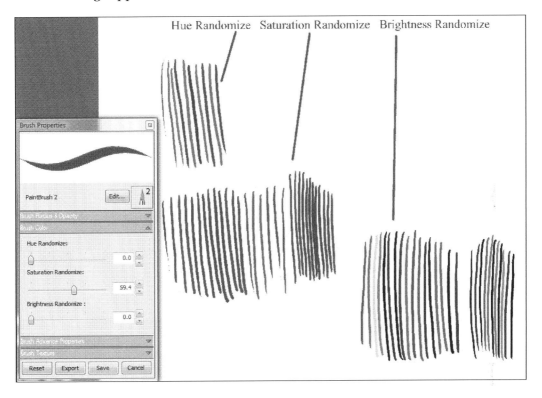

7. The **Advance Properties** window shown in the following screenshot affects the shape of your stroke. The degree of roundness and rotation in a brush will affect the tilt of the stroke and how it tapers off. The brush stroke is made up of small stamps (dots or shapes). Using the spacing slider, you can change the distance between the stamps in the strokes as shown in the following screenshot:

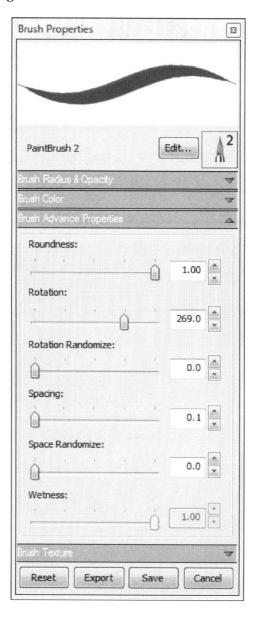

Custom texture

To capture a shape, you can either create the shape on the canvas or import an image that has the shape you want to capture. Select **Shape** or **Shape + Color** from the drop-down list in the **Brush Texture** section and click on **Capture**. An ellipse appears; place this ellipse over the shape you want to capture and click on the selection. You can adjust the size of the ellipse using the brush puck so that you can capture more or less of the shape within the ellipse area. Once you capture the shape, you can tweak the spacing, opacity, and so on to get the effect you want.

When you capture **Shape + Color**, you will not be able to use the brush with any color other than the one assigned when you created the brush.

The following screenshot shows two textures that were created by capturing a shape and then tweaking it further by changing the spacing and rotation. On the sample screenshot labeled **1**, randomize color was also selected to give an added effect to the new texture. In that same screenshot the example **2**, shows how to capture shape and color. In the **Custom Texture** field, choose the **Shape + Color** option. While using the **Shape + Color** option, the color of the brush cannot be changed. You will notice in the screenshot that the color puck reads one color but the color of the final stroke is independent of that selection. You can vary the value by placing a layer underneath the existing layer with one transparency setting and the top layer with either a higher or a lower transparency setting:

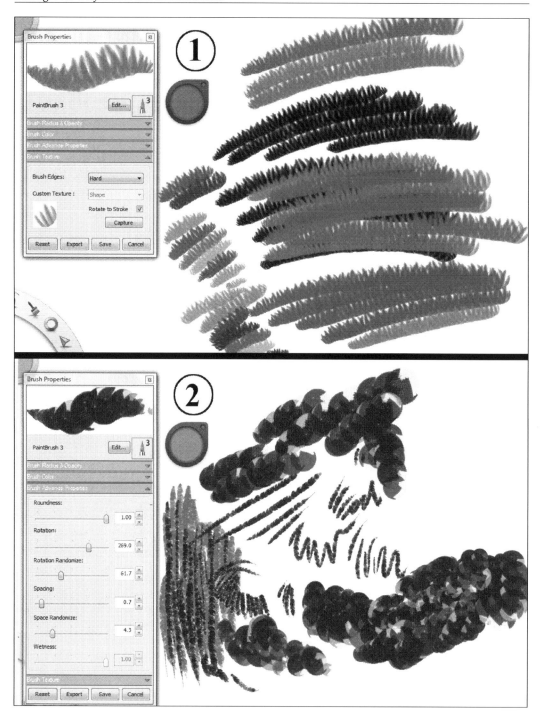

The following screenshot shows the settings for a brush created for ink work. If you want a brush for drawing fine pen and ink lines or lush brush and ink strokes, tweak the properties until you get what you want. The settings for an ink brush are shown in the following screenshot. The size and weight of the stroke can be adjusted as needed using the brush puck and pen pressure properties:

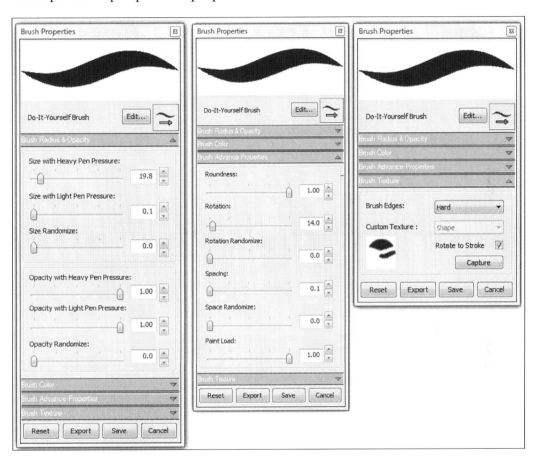

The following drawings were created using a brush with the same properties shown in the previous sections:

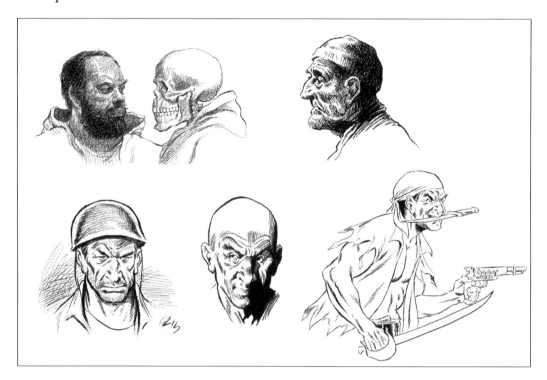

Customizing the Lagoon tab and the right-click menu

Select **Edit** from the menu bar and go to **Preferences**. You will see a pop-up window as shown in the following screenshot; select the **Lagoon** tab:

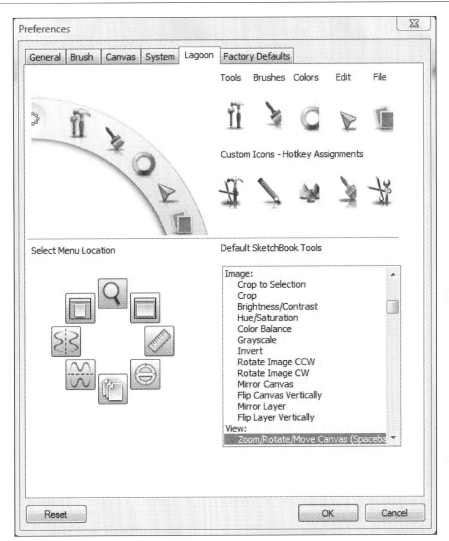

In the upper-half of the window, you will see the lagoon to the left. You can select one of the icons in the lagoon and swap the icon image with one of the images to the right of the lagoon. This will not change any of the menu items for that icon; it will only change the icon image.

To change the menu items for any of the icons in the lagoon, select the icon image from the lagoon in the upper-half of the window. The menu items for the selected icon will appear in the lower-half of the window. To the right of the menu items is a list of all the tools and brushes available in SketchBook Pro. Select one of the items from the menu and click on any of the choices in the list to swap between the tool and brush.

The tools/view menu in the lagoon has the same set of options available to you when you right-click on the screen as shown in the next screenshot. Right-click on the canvas and the tools/view options will appear on your screen so that you can quickly select the tools. For this reason, it would be advantageous to customize this option so that the tools you use the most are available by simply right-clicking on them and selecting them. Any changes made to the right-click menu will take effect after restarting SketchBook Pro.

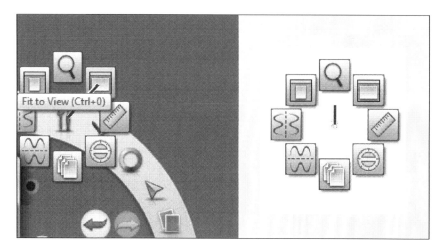

Stylus responsiveness

From the menu bar, select **Edit** and then select **Stylus Responsiveness**. The following screenshot shows the window that will pop up. By changing the position of the marker on the slider, you will customize how the stylus responds to the amount of pressure you apply to your brush stroke.

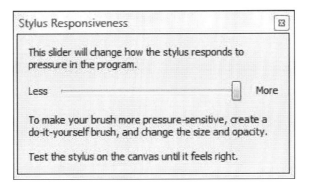

Select a brush and change the position of the marker on the slider. Test the brush on your canvas and see if you need to move the marker. Once you are satisfied with the response of the stylus on the screen, close the pop-up window.

Summary

Now that we have learned about tools, settings, and customization, it's time to start creating images. In the next chapter, we will explore making images that resemble pen and ink drawings. We will also include coloring an image imported into SketchBook Pro.

3
Creating an Image Using Pen, Ink, and Color

One of the many great things about SketchBook Pro is that you don't need a whole lot of know-how to begin making images. The interface is so familiar that you will start making successful images right off. Not that there won't always be questions of how do you do this, where do you find that, or how can you do something even better. In this chapter, we will begin to explore these questions as we apply the program to some very basic ways of creating images.

Brush choices

Because SketchBook Pro has so many brushes, there are a number of ways to create a pen, brush, or ink drawing. There's a Chisel Tip Pen, Felt Tip Pen, Ballpoint Pen, Copic Multi-liner, and a Copic Drawing Pen. All of these will give you a line similar to what you would get using those types of markers. If you are looking for something that resembles a nib pen or comic-style inking brush, then you would have to do a little tweaking of your brush properties or create a Do-It-Yourself Brush.

The Pencil tool

The Pencil tool works well as a dark ink line, although the line will be a bit soft compared to an inked line. As long as your preferences for the canvas are set at no less than 4000 for either the **Height:** or **Width:** fields and the **Resolution:** field at least at 400, the pencil line will be a very dense black. To change your preferences, on the menu bar, go to **Edit | Preferences | Canvas**. The Pencil tool will give you a quality that the marker tools lack—a more lively line that can go from thin to thick and taper off, similar in appearance to the type of line you would get from a nib pen or brush. The following screenshot shows a drawing created using the Pencil tool:

Do-It-Yourself Brush

Because an ink drawing is made up of lines, the variety of lines is the most important characteristic of this type of drawing. Not only are there many kinds of pen nibs that produce different types of lines, but you can also create different brushes that produce lines suitable to the look you would like your drawing to have. Rather than limiting yourself to the default brush choices, it would be more satisfying to create a Do-It-Yourself Brush that would suit your style. The following screenshot illustrates a suggestion for an ink brush that you can tweak to reflect your own stylistic goals:

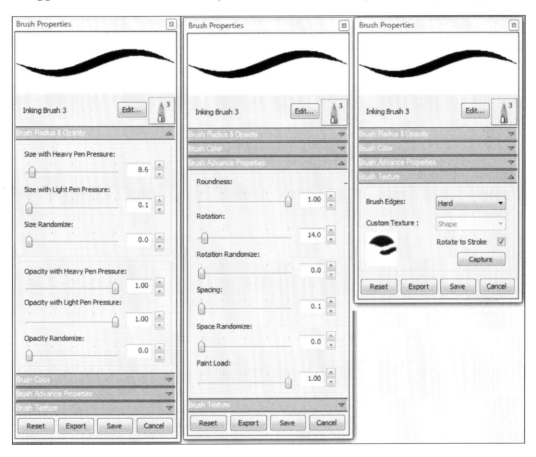

The following drawings were created with a brush using the properties just shown and are an example of the various lines and styles possible with this brush. The image in the following screenshot was made to look as though it were drawn with a pen nib:

The drawing in the following screenshot resembles a drawing done with brush and ink:

The drawing in the following screenshot uses the widest variety of line weights to create an image—from the very thick lines used in the background to thin lines used to define the faces. The variety of line weights and size are controlled with the **Brush Puck** option and pen pressure.

To add further variety to your ink drawings, you can create brushes that suit your specific style. The following is a brush that was created to simulate a Dry Brush drawing. It has the texture that resembles a brush stroke being dragged across a rough surface.

1. To create the brush, open the brush library and go to the **Texture** set.

2. To start off with a texture, click on the Camo brush as shown in the graphic.

3. Then go to the ring of dots on the upper-right corner of the texture set and click on it and then select **New Brush**.

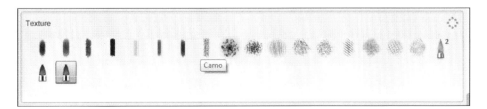

Use the settings illustrated in the following screenshot to set the properties for this brush:

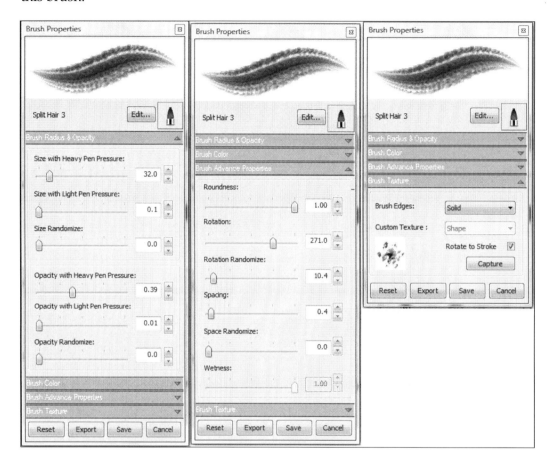

The following illustration as created with the Split Hair or Dry Brush tools. Because of the way in which the color (black) is deposited on the canvas, the lines are not as dense initially as in the other brushes. The drawing can be built-up by layering one stroke upon another to darken the value.

The brush strokes in the screenshot are made with this Dry Brush. The hatched lines and cross-hatched lines can suggest shadow, color, and texture.

You can also use a combination of brushes to create a drawing with rich darks as well as suggest values, color, and texture.

The following illustration uses both the Ink Brush and the Dry Brush tools. The Ink Brush tool was first used to establish the richest darks. Next, the Dry Brush tool was used to suggest the direction of light and shadow. Crosshatching and heavy pen pressure were used to create the darker gray areas. This helped in showing the transition from black to gray.

Coloring a drawing inked in SketchBook Pro

Once you've completed your drawing, applying color is very easy. Place a layer underneath your drawing and choose whichever tool you would like to color with. Either the Copic markers or the Airbrush tools work very well in covering the area underneath. In the following example, the Airbrush tool was used to color the ink drawing. It's good practice to keep things on separate layers, such as a hat, face, shirt, and background, so that when you have to make a change in one area, you can do so without affecting the other areas. Using layering with varying transparency also helps to change the coloring underneath, as shown in the following screenshot. Traditional painters call this glazing. To glaze in a traditional painting, you would apply a transparent wash of paint over a dry area of color. The result would be a subtle change in the color underneath. The following color swatches show the effect of glazing at varying layers of transparency. The original color of the square is in the middle and the glazes are applied to the corners.

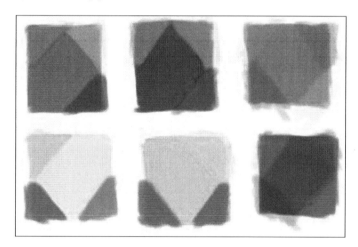

Demo 1 – the Pen, Ink, and Airbrush tools

In the following demonstration, the Ink brush is employed to create a quick sketch of an elderly gentleman. The initial inspiration for this drawing was a sketch done of a fellow passenger while travelling on the New York City Subway. One of the goals of this demonstration will be to retain the immediacy of the original sketch. The completed pen and ink drawing can be seen in the following screenshot:

The next step is to add the color.

In the following image, the layer containing the line drawing was locked so that only the areas that are drawn will be affected. The lines were gone over with the Airbrush tool, changing the color in the areas, so that it would be closer to the local color in that area.

Another layer was created and placed underneath the line drawing. The figure was colored using a combination of the Airbrush and Paintbrush tools. Another layer was created for the background and placed underneath the other layers. The Split Hair Brush tool was used, increasing the size of the brush, to quickly put in some color in the background. Lastly, a final layer was added, this time on top. On this layer, the lightest areas and accents were placed.

Demo 2 – the Pencil tool and Copic markers

The drawing of the ogre in the following screenshot was first sketched out using pencil. On that initial layer, the transparency was lowered, and a second layer was placed where the Pencil tool was used to ink the drawing as well as make whatever corrections were necessary.

By placing a layer beneath the inked drawing, we can begin to color the sketch using the Copic marker and the Pencil tool. The Pencil tool is also used for more precise coloring and the marker tool is used to cover larger areas. The only concern is putting down the local color; it's okay for the color to be uneven at this point because more color will be continually added over the whole area of the drawing. The initial background layer where I first sketched was deleted out from the drawing so that it would not be a distraction. Speaking of distractions, you'll notice from these images that I keep a lot of windows open as I work. That is just my preference. When I work with traditional materials, I like to have all my materials at hand; similarly, when I work digitally, I like to see my choices before me. Other people prefer to hide their windows and leave open only what they are currently using. The advantage to this is a bigger work area. As previously shown in this section, SketchBook Pro allows you to hide as many windows as you want according to your preference.

Here, another layer is placed over the first colored layer. The transparency is lowered on this layer to glaze color over what's underneath. With the Copic marker tools, you can add lighter colors over a darker background, as long as what you are adding is not totally white. The tool does not recognize white. If you need to add white, you can do so with the Pencil tool or any of the Brush tools. Anything totally white is held off for accents added at the end.

Warmer glazes are added using reds, ochers, and browns over the green color as well as some off-white values to lighten some areas. After adding some of these touches, the layer is merged with the one underneath it and a new layer is created with a different degree of transparency. This is done as often as needed to refine the coloring of the image.

In the final step, a layer is added as the background color. The inked layer is gone over by adding light accents, getting rid of some of the unnecessary dark lines, and making any final drawing corrections. It is a good idea to use as many layers as needed when making images in SketchBook Pro. The reason for this is when the image is saved in SketchBook's default TIFF format, and it becomes necessary to make changes, they can be done on one layer without affecting the other areas that don't need correction.

Demo 3 – coloring a scanned drawing

If you created and scanned an original drawing using pen and ink on paper, SketchBook Pro allows you to import that image. The image should be scanned in no less than 400 dpi and saved as a TIFF, JPEG, or PNG file.

Click on the add image icon in the Layers editor, as shown in the following screenshot, to import your image onto the canvas:

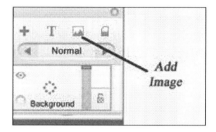

When the image is imported, the zoom/rotate/move canvas tool will be activated so that you can resize your image to fit the canvas, as in the following screenshot:

Once the image is on the canvas, go back to the Layers editor and select **Multiply** from among the blend modes. You can see this in the following screenshot of the Layers editor. This will allow SketchBook Pro to ignore the white areas so that you will be able to add color to your image.

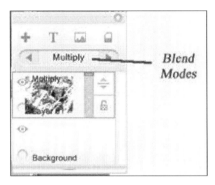

It is good practice to work from the background toward the front when coloring the image. The Bucket tool is used to add a warm color to the background. The background color will change as the image evolves.

The image is colored in the same way as the previous demonstrations. Layers are added for different elements in the picture and colored separately. More layers are added at varying transparencies to alter the color underneath.

The background color is changed and a darker color is introduced on another layer with very low transparency. This glaze shades the background color, making it less bright and less distracting.

As in the previous demos, the lightest accents are saved for the end. Adding a layer over the line drawing, some of the darker areas are brought down in value by lowering the transparency of the layer and adding a light color using the Airbrush tool. The lightest accents are then placed using the Pencil tool. The image in the following screenshot is the complete painting:

Summary

The preceding demonstration illustrated some of the ways one can develop an image in SketchBook Pro. We have really only scratched the surface on the many possible uses of the tools in the program. But choices are made according to an artist's preference. If you like, you can think of these demos as a starting point to get you to consider the tools you would use to develop your image.

In the next chapter, we will look into creating an image in the same fashion one might create an oil or acrylic painting.

4

Creating a Painting

For the most part when you are painting in SketchBook Pro, you are following the same rules and principals you would use with traditional media. There are slight differences and some advantages, but all in all, the computer is just another medium.

The following demonstrations will show how to develop a painting using SketchBook Pro. The steps used are almost exactly the same steps one would use in developing a painting using traditional materials. The exception is that one may take advantage of the tools available in SketchBook Pro. These tools include working on layers, controlling the opacity of the layers, the Lasso tool, as well as being able to use and/or create a vast array of brushes, and the ability to click on redo when you are unsatisfied with a result.

The first demonstration will be a simple subject relying on the layers and one brush to develop the image. The second demonstration will involve a more complicated composition and make use of more tools to complete the image.

Demo 1 – Painting Joshua

Our first image represents the block in stage of traditional painting. Only a general description of the light and dark shapes is indicated to give an idea of what one intends to paint. The Synthetic Coarse Angular Brush is used at this point. Throughout this first demonstration, the tool most used will be the Synthetic Coarse Angular Brush. This brush is used to give the appearance of the strokes made by a bristle brush used in oil or acrylic painting. The brush should be around size 80. I am not concerned about details here, only about the general light and dark patterns that you would see if you squint your eye while looking at an object.

Another layer is created and placed below the first one. The second layer is filled in using the Flood Fill tool (bucket shaped) to have a background color to paint on top of the previous layer.

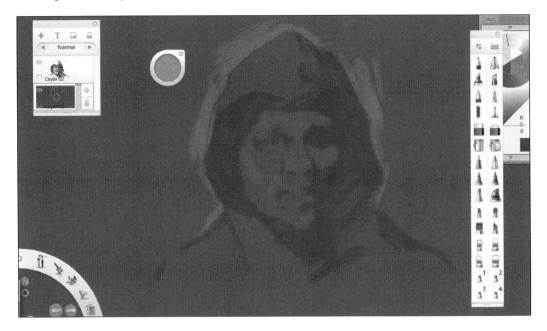

By adding layers at varying transparencies, you can continue to refine the light and dark areas. To get at the details, work from the big shapes to the smaller ones. By adding and merging the layers, you can control the values as well as both deepen the shadows and add lighter colors to bring out the forms that define the features. It's like sculpting with paint, or in this case color and value. When one is satisfied with a layer and thinks that the goals for that layer have been accomplished, merge that layer, open another layer, and continue to refine the painting. In the following screenshot, you can see the features of the face starting to take shape:

In the following screenshot, the features of the face have been established and continue to be refined. As explained in the previous steps, a layer is added with a specific goal in mind. By glazing a greenish color near the jaw and moustache area or deepening the dark areas in the hood, the layer is merged and a new one is opened as the process of refinement starts over again. The more you continue to do this, the more refined the details in the painting will be. The size of the brush is decreased as needed for finer details.

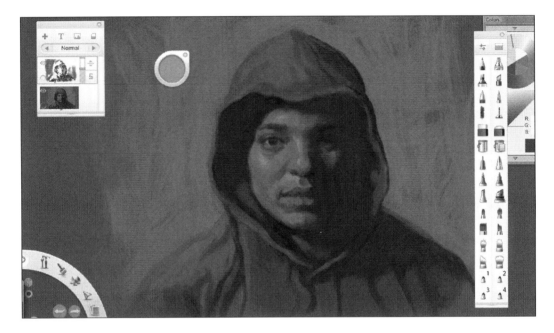

In the final stage, you can see from the screenshot, all the layers have been merged. One of the benefits of working with layers and merging them is to be able to control how the dark areas are treated. The area is not all of one color or value, so that there is a feeling of translucency and space in the areas between the head and the hood.

The final painting is as shown in the following screenshot:

Demo 2 – Creating an environment and exploring the details

In the following sections, we will explore the details of the painting of a flutist. In this second illustration, an image is placed within a fully-realized environment. One of the challenges of painting this image is the different types of textures and details involved in making a convincing image. Painting a gnarled tree, foliage, chain links, as well as the figure, are some of the different challenges in this composition. Yet all the different textures, as you will see, will be painted using a similar approach.

In the following screenshot, we see the block in stage where the concern is about the placement of different elements in the composition. Only a general indication of these is necessary. Four different layers are used to place the elements of the composition onto the canvas. The objects in these layers can be moved and resized until one is satisfied with the overall composition.

For instance, the post on the right of the figure was too tall. Selecting that layer and using the Lasso tool, the post is selected and resized to match the height of the other posts, as shown in the following screenshot:

By using a fairly large-sized Synthetic Coarse Angular Brush, the background is laid in. It's a good idea to start with the background since the colors of the environment are going to influence the colors on the main figure in the composition.

The entire composition is painted in a similar way to the previous demo, using layers and merging them with the one below it and continuing this step until the painting is finished. However, with a composition like this, where there are so many different elements in the picture, it is best to keep these elements separated on different layers. There are four layers in this painting; they are the background, the tree, the figure, and the foreground. Layers are added and merged to either enhance the painting or make the corrections, but all the different elements are kept in their own layer throughout the painting. Also, unlike the first painting, there is an added complication of rendering different textures. In this painting more tools are employed to complete the painting.

The figure

The figure is laid in using the Synthetic Coarse Angular Brush. The refinement process is the same as the previous demo, except that the details are worked up; the Pencil tool is used to refine the areas in the beard and other areas where a more crisp edge is needed. The Dry Brush that was introduced in *Chapter 3, Creating an Image Using Pen, Ink, and Color*, is also employed to give texture to the beard.

Every shape that is painted in this composition is developed in the same way. First give an indication of the shape. Paint in the big, dark, and middle value areas and continue to refine those areas as you work toward the lightest accents. This approach will work for the face, the beard, the clothing, the tree, and foliage. The only difference will be achieving the look of different textures. The best way to achieve this in SketchBook Pro is to use the best tool or tools suited for that texture. The screenshots following the description illustrates the development of the figure in the composition.

1. The face is worked on using the same process as the previous demo, only that the Pencil tool and the Synthetic Coarse Angular Brush are being switched back and forth. The Pencil tool can be more precise when putting in detail and crisper edges. At the same time, the Pencil tool has a soft line so the edges won't appear too hard.

2. The shape, value, and color of the beard are being refined using the Synthetic Coarse Angular Brush at this point. Also, the small patch of fur on his coat to the right of his head is being worked on. The darkest color of the fur is placed first, and then a middle value is indicated. Like the beard, you do not need to be concerned with individual strands but with the overall shape and value.

3. The beard, fur, face, and hat continue to be refined using the process of opening new layers and merging them, as shown in the previous demo. The Dry Brush is used on the hair, beard, and fur, and the Blur tool is introduced when the edges get too hard. The Blur tool can be found in the brush library if it is not already on your palette.

4. Using the Layers, Dry Brush, and Pencil tool, the image is refined and completed.

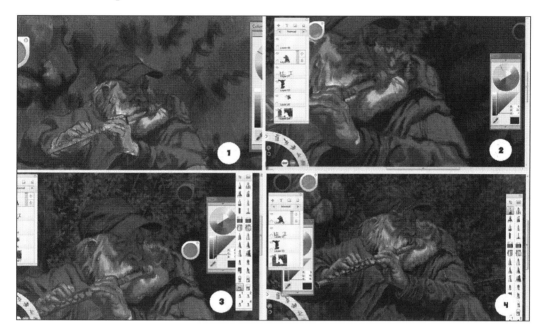

The tree

In developing the tree, you can see from the screenshots how the process went from a very general statement starting on the left to a more refined version on the right. In the process, a layer was opened up above the layer containing the tree. Varying the transparency on these additional layers, one can make corrections in value, color, and shapes and merge the layer with the one below. The Dry Brush tool is used on the final layers for getting finer details. It gives the appearance of a dry and rough brush stroke, which is perfect for the texture of the tree, as shown in the following screenshot:

The foliage

The numbers in the following steps correspond to the numbered areas in the following screenshot, and describe the progression of development of the foliage in the painting:

1. A very broad and general indication is given to the foliage behind the figure. The only concern at this stage is for the shape, and dark and middle values.

2. On the right-hand side of this image, one can see the refinement of the shape and value of the bushes before clumps of leaves are picked out from the left. Do try to stick to one lighter value at this point to keep individual leaves from jumping out of the painting and being a distraction from the main focus, which is the figure.

3. At this stage, some warmer colors are introduced on the leaves as well as a few lighter accents. A sky blue shade is also introduced to show some openings in the bushes. The brushes used are the Synthetic Coarse Angular Brush, Pencil tool, and the Dry Brush. The image is also being refined using the layers as with the rest of the painting.

4. In the final image, the values are simplified by introducing a layer at a low transparency and glazing the foliage over with a dark color. To further knock back some of the areas, we will use the Blur tool to lower the contrast in the darkest areas.

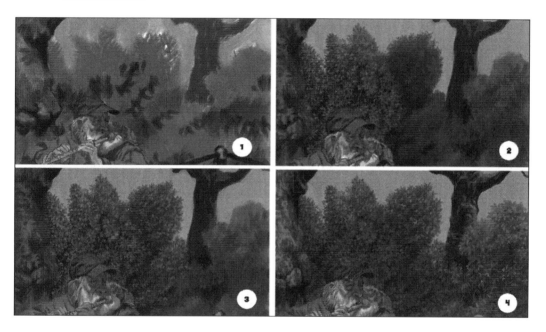

The chain link

The chain links were drawn using a simple line drawing, they were glazed over with a middle value after which the darker colors were applied, and then the lighter colors were put in to define the chains. The main definition of the links is found in the dark and middle values with the lightest accents used sparingly and being carefully placed so that the dark, middle, and light values accurately reflect how the light strikes the object. Do not get lost in trying to define each individual link. Try to explain how all these links form one chain. Keep it as simple as possible. The chain was painted using the Synthetic Coarse Angular Brush and Pencil tool. The posts were painted using the Synthetic Coarse Angular Brush, and wherever necessary the Line tool found in the toolbar was used for a straight line.

As seen in the following screenshot, the transparency in the layer containing the tree behind the posts was temporarily lowered, to make it easier to work on the chain links.

All the details and textures in the painting were built up in the same way, using the layers and utilizing the brushes and tools that work best with the texture of the objects. The following screenshot shows the painting from the initial stages to the end result using the methods described:

The final painting is as shown in the following screenshot:

Summary

As the preceding demonstrations show, SketchBook Pro can be used for developing images ranging from a quick sketch to a fully-realized painting. Using the layers and the appropriate brushes and tools, one can effectively simulate the look of a painting done in traditional media.

In the next chapter, we will discuss the file saving options for your completed images.

5
File Saving Options

Either you've finished your image and you are pretty satisfied with your piece of work, or maybe you want to bring it into another software so that you can continue to work on your project. As in any other graphics software, there are a number of file saving options in SketchBook Pro too. In this chapter, we will consider what save options are best for what you intend to do with your image.

Save options

The following is a list of the save options in SketchBook Pro along with a brief description:

- **TIFF (Tagged Image File Format)**:This is the default saving option in SketchBook Pro. The layers are retained when you save a file using this option, so you can continue working with all your layers intact. It's a good idea to keep all your layers since you may find it necessary to make corrections later. TIFF is not supported by all web browsers, so this is not a good save option if you want to post your image on the Web—the file would be too large to use on the Web anyway. It is an excellent choice if you intend to print your image.

- **JPEG (Joint Photographic Experts Group)**: This file is smaller than a TIFF because it uses a compression method that causes the image to lose some data when it is saved. It does this to create a smaller file that can be used on the Web. In some software, including SketchBook Pro, you are able to control the amount of compression and save the image to make it suitable for either the Web or for printing.

A pop-up window with a slider will appear when you select this save option as shown in the following screenshot:

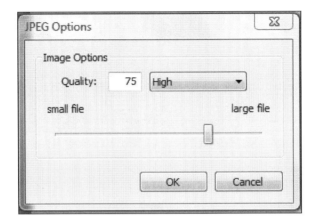

You can control the amount of compression and the quality of the image by adjusting the slider. The smaller the file, the more the compression, and the image will be of a lower quality; it will be exactly opposite for a large file. It is important to note that if you continue to save the same file in a JPEG format, the quality of file will deteriorate each time. Saving it in TIFF or PSD will prevent any loss of data. Use of the JPEG format is best for the Web because of the smaller file size.

*   **GIF (Graphics Interchange Format)**: This format is used for simple images such as diagrams, logos, and shapes. It is also widely used on the Web to create a simple animation. A GIF retains the transparency of the areas surrounding the image. This is an image format recommended for very simple web graphics but not for printing.

- **PNG (Portable Network Graphics)**: Like a GIF file, a PNG file is also used for animation because it preserves the transparency of the image. PNG files are of better quality than GIF files and they result in larger files. PNG is also a better quality file than JPEG—the file can be a smaller one than a JPEG file with no loss of data. Where other file formats will fill the blank areas in your image with white, these file formats leave the area transparent as well as preserve different levels of transparency within the image. To take advantage of the transparency in both GIF and PNG images, make sure that you have **Transparent background** checked in **Preferences** as seen in the following screenshot:

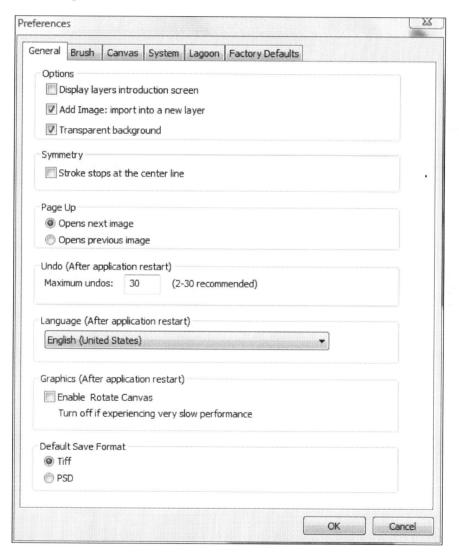

A PNG file does not always show up the same on all graphics software—some areas may appear darker than you intended. This file format was designed to work best in web browser applications. In the next screenshot, you can see the transparent background around the image:

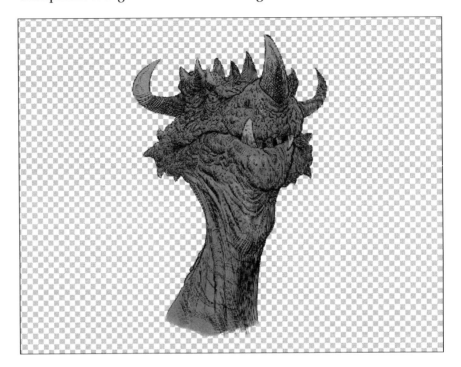

- **BMP (Windows Bitmap)**: Bitmaps can be high-quality images but they are also huge files, and there is virtually no difference in the quality when compared to TIFF files. Moreover, TIFFs are more widely used, especially on computers that do not run on Windows.

- **PSD (Photoshop Document)**: PSD is, of course, Adobe Photoshop's default file format. Saving a file in this format will preserve your layers when you import the file into Photoshop. TIFF files will not preserve the layers outside SketchBook Pro. Saving in the PSD file format will allow you to continue working in Photoshop, which allows you to continue working on your image using the options in this software. The following illustration was created in SketchBook Pro 6 and completed using the watercolor filter in Photoshop:

- **SketchBook iOS (Mac)**: This file format is available on Macintosh computers, so your image can be saved and opened in the SketchBook Pro IOS Version. It preserves your layers so that you can continue to work on it using your iPad.

- **Pixlr PXD (Pixlr design file format)**: If you don't have Photoshop, Pixlr Editor is a free online photo editor similar to Photoshop. It uses the PXD format. You can save your image in PXD and open it in the Pixlr Editor where you can further develop your image.

Importing an image to Flash

If you use Flash and want to create an image in SketchBook Pro in order to import it into a Flash project, you can save your image either as a GIF or PNG file. Flash has a lot of other importing options as well. You can create an image in SketchBook Pro with all the moving parts on different layers and import it to Flash. The layers and layer order will be retained. The following screenshot is a simple image created in SketchBook Pro, saved as a PSD file, and imported onto the stage in Flash:

Importing an image to Photoshop

With the exception of SketchBook IOS and Pixlr PXD, all of these files can be opened in Photoshop. This extends the options that you have for creating your image as you can use all of the tools available in Photoshop. Exploring the filters in Photoshop can enhance your image. As was shown in an earlier image, you can use the watercolor filter in Photoshop to give your image the look of having been done in watercolors. The following is an illustration created in SketchBook Pro 6 and brought into Photoshop where some of the filters were applied. The result of applying the filters makes the image appear as a watercolor image. The original image can be seen as follows:

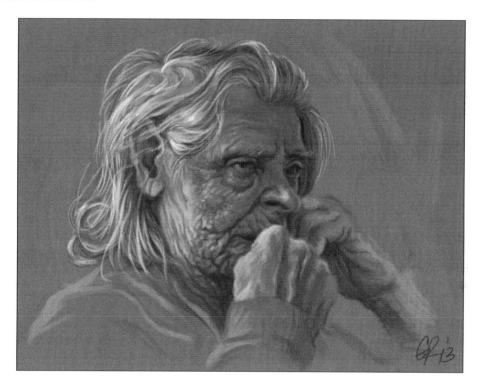

The image was saved as TIFF and brought into Photoshop as seen in the next screenshot. As you can see from the image, the first filter applied is the **Paint Daubs** filter. This is to simplify the details in the image. The settings are adjusted and once you are satisfied, click on **OK**:

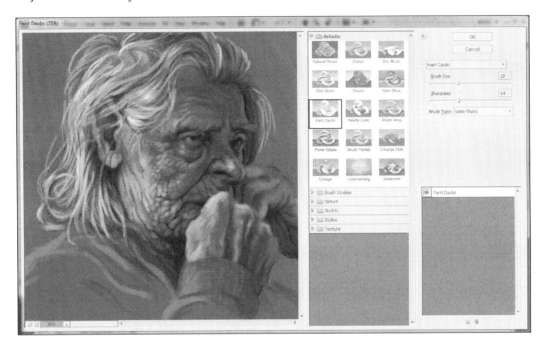

In the following screenshot, the filter options are applied once again. This time the watercolor filter is selected. The settings are adjusted again and once the image looks just about right, **OK** is clicked. Depending on the original image, it may take more than one pass with this filter to get the desired effect. The following screenshot shows the first pass:

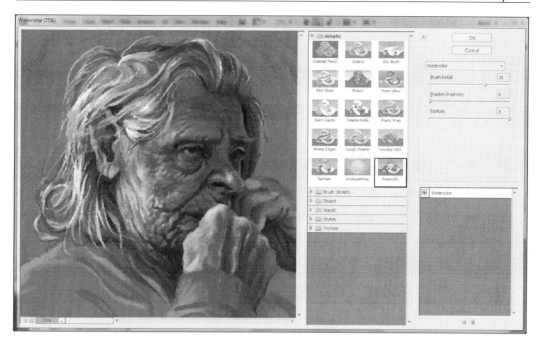

The window is closed and the second pass is applied with the same settings as the first. The resulting image gives the desired effect as shown in the next screenshot:

Because the filter can make the dark shades too dark, you may want to adjust the levels in your image as seen in the next screenshot:

Finally, here's the final image:

Summary

In this chapter we have seen that SketchBook Pro has all the tools you would need in order to create a satisfactory image, but by exporting your image, you can take advantage of the options and tools in other software programs too. We have just scratched the surface of SketchBook Pro with the examples in this chapter. The best thing to do is explore and experiment with as many software as you can.

In the next chapter we will discuss some tricks and tips that will help in you in the process of creating your image.

6
Tips and Tricks

As with any software, constant use helps build a system of best practice. Of course, a lot of this may be a personal work habit rather than a universal one, but experience is worth giving a listen to. Someone else's methods can be adapted, tweaked, and made personal or can be totally discarded in favor of one's own approach. This chapter offers some helpful tips and advice in using SketchBook Pro 6.

Tablets

To get the full benefit or experience while using SketchBook Pro, one must realize that the software was developed with pressure sensitive tablets in mind. Therefore, one of the best tips for using SketchBook Pro is to get a tablet. The most effective maker of these tablets is most probably Wacom. To get the maximum possible use and experience with SketchBook Pro, it is recommended that you purchase the best tablet you can afford. The Wacom tablets allow you to set shortcuts on the pen and tablet buttons. Some of the functions that can be set include right-click, the *Alt* key (Windows), *command* (Mac), scroll, and zoom. There is also a SketchBook Pro app that can be used on android tablets and iPad. For these, you can purchase a pressure sensitive pen or stylus.

Mirror canvas

There is a trick that artists used when they wanted to see what corrections needed to be made in their drawing. They would hold up their drawings or paintings to a mirror and the reversed image would reveal all the drawing faults in the piece. You can flip your drawing in SketchBook Pro 6 for this very same purpose. Go to the menu bar and then navigate to **Image | Mirror Canvas** to flip your image. It is always a good idea to check your drawing this way. It allows you to make whatever corrections are needed before the public can see your work. The following screenshot shows a drawing that was mirrored to reveal an awkwardly drawn helmet.

The drawing was corrected with the use of Layers and SketchBook Pro's Symmetry tools.

Making corrections

One of the beauties of SketchBook Pro is that there is more than one way to accomplish a task. When making corrections, keep in mind that you have more than one way of doing this. There are the obvious Undo/Redo and Eraser options. The Lasso tool allows you to select and either cut, move, or resize a specific object. You can also use the layers as tracing paper, making corrections on a layer placed above your image and erasing what's underneath, and then merging the layers. Having many options comes in handy because one option might require more work than the other. If you decide to use the layers as tracing paper, it would require more work to make your corrections; however, using the layers allow for unlimited undos. If you choose the Undo option, you must remember that you have a limit of 30 undos. It's also a good idea to save your document at different intervals in case you want to return to an earlier version. SketchBook Pro automatically names your document when you select **Save As...**, so it creates a new file each time, whereas selecting **Save** will update the current file.

Painting outside the lines

The Layers and Corrections options allow you to make what would otherwise be disastrous mistakes if you were working with traditional materials. For instance, since you are making your image on different layers and are hopefully coloring your line drawing in the layer underneath, you don't have to worry about painting within the line; it's not a coloring book. You can either erase the areas you don't want to include in your image or paint over that area in another layer. The images in the following two screenshots show a drawing that was first colored and then cleaned up with the Eraser tool.

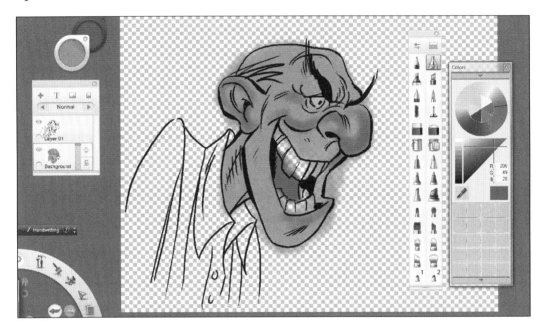

After cleaning up the drawing, you can lock the layer, and as you continue to work on that layer, only the areas that were already painted will be affected by any changes you make. You can also duplicate the layer, set it to the desirable transparency, lock it, and continue to work on the image without straying from the lines. The following screenshot shows the complete image created using these layering techniques:

Summary

There is a great deal of information regarding SketchBook Pro on the Web. Many people are willing to share what they have learned and offer a great deal of helpful tips. Autodesk (the makers of SketchBook Pro) has a number of tutorials on their website. These are offered by professional designers, illustrators, and cartoonists and are extremely helpful. In addition, YouTube has quite a few videos and sites likes deviantART, has groups dedicated to SketchBook Pro. These sites allow you to look over an artist's shoulder as they are working, which is a good way of learning.

With all the information that is out there, you have more than enough information to master the software in a short time. The program is very easy to learn, so intuitive, and addictive. It allows you more time to concentrate on mastering your drawing and painting abilities while exploring the software. Its ease of use makes it a great application for professionals and hobbyists alike. The tips and tricks offered in this chapter and throughout the book are just the tip of the iceberg. In no time, you will be offering your own tips as you become more comfortable with SketchBook Pro.

There is an additional chapter, *Gallery of Images*, which can be downloaded from the PACKT website. The chapter contains a gallery of images created in SketchBook Pro along with a brief description. This gallery of images shows how we use the program for our personal work and is meant to inspire the reader to create similar, and hopefully better works using SketchBook Pro.

Index

About Packt Publishing

Packt, pronounced 'packed', published its first book "*Mastering phpMyAdmin for Effective MySQL Management*" in April 2004 and subsequently continued to specialize in publishing highly focused books on specific technologies and solutions.

Our books and publications share the experiences of your fellow IT professionals in adapting and customizing today's systems, applications, and frameworks. Our solution based books give you the knowledge and power to customize the software and technologies you're using to get the job done. Packt books are more specific and less general than the IT books you have seen in the past. Our unique business model allows us to bring you more focused information, giving you more of what you need to know, and less of what you don't.

Packt is a modern, yet unique publishing company, which focuses on producing quality, cutting-edge books for communities of developers, administrators, and newbies alike. For more information, please visit our website: www.packtpub.com.

Writing for Packt

We welcome all inquiries from people who are interested in authoring. Book proposals should be sent to author@packtpub.com. If your book idea is still at an early stage and you would like to discuss it first before writing a formal book proposal, contact us; one of our commissioning editors will get in touch with you.

We're not just looking for published authors; if you have strong technical skills but no writing experience, our experienced editors can help you develop a writing career, or simply get some additional reward for your expertise.

Instant GIMP Starter [Instant]

ISBN: 978-1-78216-034-2   Paperback: 80 pages

Learn the basicsof GIMP through practical examples

1. Learn something new in an Instant!
    A short, fast, focused guide delivering
    immediate results

2. Use GIMP features to draw and color images

3. Make a precise infographic

4. Compose multiple pictures in an image

Blender 2.5 HOTSHOT

ISBN: 978-1-84951-310-4   Paperback: 332 pages

Challenging and fun projects that will push your
Blender skills to the limit

1. Exciting projects covering many areas:
    modeling, shading, lighting, compositing,
    animation, and the game engine

2. Strong emphasis on techniques and
    methodology for the best approach to
    each project

3. Utilization of many of the tools available
    in Blender 3D for developing moderately
    complex projects

4. Clear and concise explanations of working in
    3D, along with insights into some important
    technical features of Blender 3D

Please check **www.PacktPub.com** for information on our titles

Mastering Adobe Premiere Pro CS6 Hotshot

ISBN: 978-1-84969-478-0   Paperback: 284 pages

Take your video editing skills to new and exciting levels with eight fantastic projects

1. Discover new workflows and the exciting new features of Premiere Pro CS6

2. Take your video editing skills to exciting new levels with clear, concise instructions (and supplied footage)

3. Explore powerful time-saving features that other users don't even know about!

4. Work on actual real-world video editing projects such as short films, interviews, multi-cam, special effects, and the creation of video montages

Mastering Adobe Captivate 6

ISBN: 978-1-84969-244-1   Paperback: 476 pages

Create professional SCORM-complaint eLearning content with Adobe Captivate

1. Step by step tutorial to build three projects including a demonstration, a simulation and a random SCORM-compliant quiz featuring all possible question slides

2. Enhance your projects by adding interactivity, animations, sound and more

3. Publish your project in a wide variety of formats enabling virtually any desktop and mobile devices to play your e-learning content

4. Deploy your e-Learning content on a SCORM or AICC-compliant LMS

Please check **www.PacktPub.com** for information on our titles

Printed in Great Britain
by Amazon